5 Reasons Why Most Teachers Can't Cope With Your Child With Special Needs

And
What You Can Do About It

By Soli Lazarus

Published by

The Endless Bookcase Ltd.

71 Castle Road, St Albans, Hertfordshire, England, AL1 5DQ.

www.theendlessbookcase.com

Printed Edition

Also available in multiple e-book formats via The Endless Bookcase website, Amazon, Nook and Kobo.

Printed in the United Kingdom

First Printing 2016, Reprinted 2017, 2019.

Copyright © Soli Lazarus 2016, 2019.

All rights reserved

ISBN: 978-1-908941-89-3

Disclaimer

There is no deliberate intention to discredit any professional, school or institution in this publication. All names have been changed to protect identity and confidentiality.

Dedication

To Styx who supports me and inspires me every day. To David and Rosie who make me smile and make me proud.

Who Is This Book Aimed At?

I have written this mainly for parents or carers who are struggling on a daily basis. Battling with schools and the 'system'. Mums (and of course dads) with children with special needs who have had to become warriors.

I hope too that professionals will read this and get inspired. And who knows - maybe I'll get my book seen all the way in Parliament where some real change could happen.

Contents

Who Is This Book Aimed At?.. i

Introduction - The System Is Broken iv

How To Use This Book:.. xi

#1 Peer Groups Are Lumped Together............................ 1

#2 Creativity Is Stifled 17

#3 Schools Can Damage Our Children's Emotional And Mental Health 27

#4 Targets Matter Too Much.. 45

#5 There's A Real World Out There 53

Conclusion - Together We Can Bring About Change 63

About The Author.. 69

Resources Available From Yellow Sun 72

Connect With Yellow Sun 73

References.. 74

Introduction - The System Is Broken

School.

What does that word conjure up for you?

For me, school was a happy place.

I am still in touch with many of my school friends some 50 years later and that makes me smile. My memories of my primary school are vivid. It was a big, old Victorian building where I walked from home on my own, going via the sweet shop and buying Bazooka Joes and Black Jacks for one penny.

Girls and boys had their separate entrances and played on separate playgrounds. Boys football, girls skipping. (I grew up in a different non-pc world). We hung upside down on monkey bars over a concrete carpet. The staffroom was a pit of smoke with teachers laughing and chattering. If you dared to knock on the Headmaster's door you would be greeted by a stern nod and a mumble. We cowered away from the witch who lived in the house overlooking our playground.

In the classroom, teachers were plonked at their desks with a snake of children queuing quietly for attention. We piled into the hall where we would all watch 'Tom's Midnight Garden' on a tiny television that was stored in a cabinet on wheels. Highlight for me was Junior Disco Club on a Friday lunchtime where we were allowed to wear our flares. Wahoo! I loved school.

Fast forward to my experience as a parent.
My son has ADHD and his primary school experience was a stark contrast to mine. He was in constant trouble and in his own words felt "lonely and isolated, left out and miserable". He would always be by himself in the playground and would fabricate reasons why he had to go the Medical Room just so he wouldn't be alone.

He was also a very angry little boy. He would steal from people's pencil cases just to get attention. How sad is that? On top of that he took medication, which in hindsight didn't suit him either (I know it suits some so I am not anti-medication). Stage one he felt high as a kite; stage 2 he felt like a zombie. He was 'statemented' which meant he had a support assistant. Years later we found out that although she was wonderful and got him through academically, he absolutely hated it as she was like a shadow and a constant reminder that he was different. He had no friends, no birthday parties, no play dates.

And me? I'd stand in the playground at the end of the day watching my little boy come out, head down, bedraggled, on his own. Invariably I'd be called over to speak to the teacher about another 'incident'. The other parents didn't want to know me either. Having a son with special needs was obviously infectious. They didn't want to catch anything. So like my son, I was excluded from coffee mornings and social nights out. It was tough for us all.

And now?
School for me is where I have spent my whole adult working life. For 30 years I have been a primary class teacher and now teaching mainly children with special needs. I was an Inclusion Specialist and Assistant Special Educational Needs Co-ordinator (SENCO) in a large primary school in London. Over the years I've seen systems change and then come full circle back to

the beginning again. Go figure. Governments have come and gone with their crazy and sometimes innovative ideas.

I've had to teach myself how to use the new-fangled interactive white board without my stress levels going through the ceiling. I've worked with some incredible people who are extremely dedicated to their profession. I've had some wonderful experiences over the many years; I've taught so many beautiful children and laughed and cried. I've witnessed the gorgeous moments when a child 'gets it' and I've experienced the lows of supporting vulnerable children from abusive backgrounds. We've been on brilliant educational trips, the most rewarding and memorable are residential school journeys where children who are trapped in the classroom feel liberated and blossom as leaders and free thinkers.

I love what I do.
But not all of what I do.
This book will highlight the frustrations I feel about a system which to me at times seems broken. There are so many fabulous aspects to our system - external

services such as Speech Therapy, Occupational Therapy, and Educational Psychologists.

Yet with hosts of innovative ideas, great Heads and outstanding teachers, many of our special children still fail to reach their full potential.

So I present five reasons why I think our primary school system is failing our special children*.

I feel this is a system that caters for the bright, motivated, atypical child.

It was reported in 2014 that 17.9%[1] of school aged children were identified as having a 'special need'. This means about five children in your child's class today will have some kind of 'need' that requires differentiation in approach or resources.
But are schools successfully catering for the needs of all our special children?

In June 2016, a survey carried by The Key[2] called for increased funding of pupils with special needs or disabilities (SEND) in mainstream classrooms. So there we have it. Factual evidence that there is not enough money going into schools to support our most needy.

Our special children - who need modifications, tolerance, understanding and maybe just a little TLC - often get pushed to the side.
Not due to lack of care but due to lack of effective teacher training in special needs.
And the effect of this? Disruptive children who are under-achieving with low self-esteem and family life that is challenging with parents who are exhausted.

Frustrated that the needs of our gorgeous special children were not being met, and to support struggling parents, I set up my consultancy Yellow Sun. My aim is to give parents a voice to challenge what is going on in our schools and to support them through the despair and loneliness of fighting the system. I want to give warrior mums and dads a battle plan so they don't feel so alone.

Sounds familiar? Read on….

*For the purposes of this book, I refer to our 'special children' to include children who have dyslexia, dyspraxia, dyscalculia, ADHD, ADD, autism, Asperger's, developmental delay, specific learning difficulties or any other syndrome that causes difficulties in learning or behaviour.

I am using the pronoun 'he' throughout this book for ease of reading - yet I am fully aware that many of our special children are girls.

How To Use This Book:

Look out for these little pictures:

 Soli's having a rant

 What you must insist should be happening in school

 What you can do at home to help your child

 A true story

 To quote someone famous

 So in conclusion

Peer Groups Are Lumped Together

Where else do we have to spend six hours a day with people exactly our own age and then are expected to be at exactly the same academic level?
I'll tell you where - nowhere.

Look around you at your work place, your group of friends, your family get togethers. We're all different ages - contributing with our various skills and talents. No one is saying "ooh you're 36 and really you should know the difference between a progressive tense and a perfect tense and what are you doing hanging round with a 23 year old?". Isn't it more important that at 36 you're a good person, contributing to society and are emotionally well?

Yet at school - which is the most important institution we'll ever belong to - we lump together children of exactly the same age and expect them to be roughly at the same academic level. But with hugely different backgrounds, experiences, culture, language, needs and abilities. That would be ok if we didn't compare these children to one another and then publish the results. But we do and that (to quote our American friends) sucks.

To make matters worse, classmates actually may be nearly a whole year older. A child who will be 5 in August will be in the same academic year as a child who will turn 6 in September. Yet we are forced to compare these children to one another, make judgements and collect data about academic progress.

Children develop at different rates. Anyone involved in education knows that. Yet data is collected and collated. Senior management teams are pressurised by local and central Government to improve standards. So the outcome is to push, push, push.

Booster groups have been setup to move children on and to pre-teach, to go over noun phrases, practice times tables. All very good, I hear you say. Our children need these basic skills. You're right, they do. And our teachers are cramming in as much as they can within the constraints of a lesson.

But these booster groups may take place during topic lessons. So children who have struggled in lessons and not achieved the desired level, have to miss out on music, geography, history, RE, art, technology, computer, drama, and in some cases PE. An horrendous situation.

But why are some children not achieving the levels that the Government is expecting our children to reach?

Are the levels too high? Almost certainly. The curriculum in the academic year 2015 to 2016 was 'upgraded' by the Conservative Government[3] led by Prime Minister David Cameron. Now all children had to acquire the knowledge and skills of the year group above. In other words, a Y3 child now had to be at the standard of a Y4 child in all areas of the curriculum. Crazy right?

Great for the bright, motivated child but what about our special children?

So this is the scenario: our special children who are already struggling with the curriculum now have to work at a level that previously was being taught to the year group above. They then have to be 'boosted' so miss out on lessons that perhaps they would have excelled at.

It's no wonder I think schools are failing our special children.

I'm not suggesting that schools shouldn't be organised as they are. It would be quite ridiculous to group children in anything other than age. Can you imagine the despair of a 14-year old if he was academically matched to a 9-year old? Age grouping on the whole is a sensible way to impart knowledge on a national scale. We need a National Curriculum and yes we even need to know roughly what our children should be able to do once they leave school.

But what we need to do is to make sure all needs are catered for. And that means adapting the curriculum to suit our children rather than in a blind panic teach adverbial phrases because that's what we should be doing in Week 3 Term 2.

Schools ideally can be a wonderful place to expose our children to new experiences and ideas. But we must insist that our schools allow all children to learn at their own level and are mindful that each child has individual needs. A tough ask for a teacher with 30 pupils, yet it is our duty as parents to protect our special children in all areas of their lives. And if that means being seen as a 'pushy' parent, so be it. However in my experience, the more parents are on-board with their child's learning, the more likelihood of success.

With that said, at every opportunity ask to see your child's books.

Things to also look out for:
- Differentiated work - not all children should be given the same work. Our special children should have work adapted so that they achieve and feel successful
- Writing frames - boxes on the paper to help organise a piece of writing
- Coloured paper used for writing or reading a block of text - imperative if they have visual difficulties or dyslexia
- Specialist or enlarged font such as Open Dyslexic
- Copy of instructions on a sheet in front of the child rather than copy from the whiteboard
- Word banks, word mats or specialist word processor programme such as Clicker[4]
- Tape recorders or sound buttons to help your child remember a sentence that then needs to be written
- Practical maths equipment such as Numicon[5], large numbered dice, number lines, 100 squares
- Sensory equipment may be needed such as weighted blanket, wobble cushion, fidget toy, chewy bracelet

By the way, a little word about Clicker. I love it. It is a brilliant software that is now being used in schools and at home to help with writing and reading. It is a really fun and engaging package that makes work achievable and fun – even for the children with the most challenging learning difficulties. I have run many training sessions on it and teachers pick up on my expertise and my enthusiasm and report back at how successful it is. I have appeared on their website as a 'Success Story'. I'm super excited about it. As a bonus if you want to buy it to use at home, go onto the Clicker website, write Yellow Sun at checkout and you'll get a 5% discount.

Have a look again at the list above.
If there is no evidence of these things happening in school, ask why not. First port of call is the class teacher. Make a convenient time to talk, most probably after school. Don't be afraid to suggest these things. A teacher may not have come across a child like yours before. So she (or he) may be grateful for the suggestions. On the other hand you may get ignored.

In which case, book an appointment to see the Special Needs Co-ordinator (SENCO) and again politely suggest some of the above techniques or equipment that could be used with your child.

If no joy here, next step a meeting with the Head and perhaps the Chair of Governors. Contact details will be on the school's website or local council. Take along a friend or colleague to give you moral support. I am not suggesting for one minute that you approach any of these meetings with anything other than quiet reserve, dignity, politeness but definitely with a steely bloody-minded resolve.

It is up to us to get everything our children need. Do not be fobbed off. If he misbehaves at school it is because the right strategies have not been put in place.

Pre-empt the behaviour and you won't be called in to have a meeting about exclusion. Instead you'll be called in to talk about how talented he is. How brilliant would that be?

Give your child a break when he comes home from school - literally! Decide together when would be the best time to tackle homework - after a short TV time, after a snack or straight away.

Homework should be independent work for about 20 mins.
If he is struggling and you are having to teach him then stop, go back to school and speak to the class teacher and insist that he is given suitable, differentiated work that is consolidating what he's already been taught at school. It should not be stressful for him or you! Use a 'how do I feel' thermometer and if he is expressing that he is 'feeling slightly angry', then keep your distance until it goes down to 'feeling calm'.

The best and most fulfilling learning is through play. Games and puzzles are fab. Download or buy board games. Google 'fun activities at home for children' - you'll be amazed at the array of websites out there in the world wide web.

I'd like you to have instant access to some free downloadable games I have made. They are my gift to you. Go to the back of this book in the reference section for website details.[6]

Join Pinterest – there are tons of ideas how to keep our children amused with everyday objects. Games for learning maths, spelling, reading. Make learning fun.

A fantastic way to encourage your dyslexic or reluctant child to read is to use kindle (or equivalent) audio books. Amazon[7] have an audio option called Audible which reads a downloaded book. Buy a comfy pair of headphones and your child can actually flip between listening and then reading the book himself. How brilliant is that?

Another great idea is to activate the sub-titles on the tv. So when he's watching his favourite programme he'll be reading without even being aware.

After school clubs. Decide the ones that really add something to your child's life. If it is somewhere else where there are rules and boundaries he can't cope with, then forget it. He'll be tired and exhausted after coping with the constraints of school - he really doesn't need this repeated in his 'leisure' time. You may think football/drama/piano/swimming is what you should be sending him to - but have a good hard look at how this club is being run. Usually the leaders of these clubs have very little knowledge or understanding of special needs.

Better to find an institution such as Chickenshed Inclusive Theatre[8]. This is an amazing theatre company that runs workshops and stages the most incredible productions featuring dance, drama, original music. They cater for all ages and abilities and include children and adults with the most profound and challenging difficulties seamlessly into their wonderful productions. Go and see a performance if you're anywhere near London – you'll be spell bound I promise.

My son was a member of Chickenshed – he had unceremoniously been asked to leave numerous clubs including music, football, cubs. But at Chickenshed he was accepted and nurtured. We now have fabulous memories of him singing and performing on stage. He also (mum showing off time – forgive me) appeared at the Royal Albert Hall with the singer Gabrielle, sang at Stringfellows nightclub (a charity event for children) and sang with a 100 voices in The Mall, London to celebrate the Queen Mother's 100th birthday.

Find the right activity and your child can succeed.

Another fantastic organisation is Penniwells Horse Riding for the Disabled[9] who actively embrace special needs. I personally organise twelve children from my school to ride there weekly. Children with autism and Down's syndrome who cannot cope or communicate effectively within the classroom, seem to magically transform once they are riding a horse. Not to mention the sing-song they have in the mini-bus on the way to the stables. This experience is a springboard for so many other activities back at school and makes it an invaluable experience.

So you just need to search the internet and find something near you that will cater for your child's needs and interests. It's out there. As Dory says 'just keep swimming'. Just keep searching.

Screen time. I know it's a great motivator and keeps him quiet for 10 minutes - but try and limit the time he is on his tablet/phone/iPad/laptop/TV. Plan your day using visual resources and a grid. Decide together how much time to spend on the screen and when to stop. Use rewards and sand timers if necessary. Make sure the next thing you want your child to do is desirable. If it's to do a chore, you're heading for a battle. If it's to come and build a Lego tower to touch the ceiling, you'll more likely get a willing participant.

James was a fantastic runner. Give him a track and a pair of running shoes, you wouldn't see him for dust. During Sports Day his classmates screamed his name in jubilation. James beamed with pride. But in the confines of the classroom it was a different story. James had severe learning difficulties, so much so that in Year 4 he was still working at Year 1 curriculum. Despite many interventions James made very slow progress. We encouraged James to join a running club where he would enjoy success and feel really good about himself. He could see clearly that there was a huge gap in his understanding between himself and his peers and so it was vital to find something where James could shine. I'm eagerly awaiting the day when I see James running with a TeamGB vest and a big fat smile.

The actor Channing Tatum talks openly about his struggles with dyslexia and ADHD. Yet he only felt of any worth once he left the institution of school.
"I have never considered myself a very smart person, for a lot of reasons. Not having early success on that one path messes with you."

The businessman and entrepreneur Richard Branson wrote "If anyone ever puts you down for having dyslexia, don't believe them. Being dyslexic can actually be a big advantage, and it has certainly helped me."

Traditional schooling, National Curriculum and age grouping is here to stay. Yet our special children can be given a huge variety of strategies and resources that make learning accessible. We can help them at home to break out of the constraints of the classroom and give them back the element of fun. Success is definitely possible.

Creativity Is Stifled

Our Governments are very keen to compare UK academic progress to other countries in order to justify teaching to an extremely high standard.

	Rank	Score
Shanghai	1	
Singapore	2	
Hongkong	3	
UK	26	

Source OECD [10] Not to scale. For illustrative purposes only

So look who's top. Shanghai (China does not participate as a country), Singapore and Hong Kong. For us to compete with Asia we are forcing our children to become little automatons, rote learning and be very well practiced in taking tests. We've all seen the footage of children in Asian countries rote learning and reciting tables - but is this what we want for any of our children let alone our special children?

Great if this is a child's way of learning - we all have different learning styles. I am a very visual learner - I need to see things in colour and love lists and videos to explain an instruction. Others are auditory learners and only have to listen to information and it will be processed. Many of our special children are kinaesthetic learners, which means that have to actually make something or touch something for a concept to be understood.

Some of our special children can rote learn - yet ask them to use this information to solve a problem and our children would come unstuck. And so fail in a test.

Some of our special children are extremely creative and can tell you a really detailed description of a fabulous day out. Language will be rich and exciting. But ask him to formally write it out as part of a lesson and the outcome will be very different. The language will become stilted and formulaic. He'll write the word 'big' because he can't write 'ginormous'. So we are stifling creativity. We are lessening the opportunities at school for exploring creativity as the focus is on excellence in the core subjects.

Some of children flourish on the sports field, yet are not given the opportunity to be in the school team due to their 'disruptive' behaviour in class. But we need to question why is there disruptive behaviour?

Perhaps the lesson has not been adapted sufficiently and that his needs are not being met, he is not listened to and feels frustrated. Then schools are taking away the kudos of excelling in the school football team, netball team, running field. I know of boys who have been chucked out of the school football team because of their behaviour. This absolutely cannot be right. Let's get it right for him in the classroom then the rest will follow.

What about the brilliant artist? How are his skills demonstrated to his classmates? Unless the teacher gives opportunities for freedom of expression then these talents will be left untapped. And what about our children who are fabulous mimics or singers or actors or piano players. Our children who can cook up a scrumptious meal in the kitchen. It is imperative that the teacher is aware of these incredible skills and then uses them as a springboard to support their learning.

And isn't the world amazing because we all have unique qualities. How dull and boring if we were all the same! Can you imagine a debate where everyone agrees and no one has a unique opinion? Yet this is what the institution of school is foisting upon our children. To become little people who use the same vocabulary or use the same method to solve a problem. Where are the opportunities for free thinking and exploration?

Schools are not set up for our children to be creative. They are set up for them to obey, be silent, sit still, produce near identical work. Children quickly learn to give teachers what teachers expect. In this bizarre world, a child is praised and given a top score because a piece of work includes all the components demanded. Check list; commas, apostrophes, noun phrase, inverted comma. Tick, tick, tick, tick. But goodness me how stifled, bland and boring this work is.

We must be mindful that we don't overlook talents of our special children. Teachers sometimes are so caught up in what he can't do, rather than be amazed by what he can actually do extremely well.

Ask the class teacher what opportunities your child has to explore his creativity?

This could be:

- To join a dance, drama, lego, painting, cooking club in the lunch-time or after school
- The teacher to give your child massive praise when he achieves something creative - a model, a dance, a piece of drama. Ask for photos to be taken if possible and these can be used to make a 'Brilliant Me' book
- Ask if it's really necessary to take your child out of topic lessons for booster. (if the correct tools were implemented in the lesson - see above - maybe he wouldn't need a booster group...)
- Suggest that your child record his work through different medium such as laptop, photos, drawing, voice recorder, drama. I do appreciate this is not always possible but during topic work particularly the written word is not always necessary. Ask if he can be allowed to choose how he presents his work
- If your child has a particular talent, make sure the teacher enhances it. Let him show the class or whole school what he can do. Your child who is a great little dramatist should be given an appropriate role in an assembly or school play

- Make sure the class teacher knows your child's learning style - then plays to his strengths

Find the one thing that he is successful at and make sure he has every opportunity to shine.

Have less focus on learning spellings and more on making a mud pie in the garden.
Incorporate learning and homework in fun and imaginative ways.
Demonstrate how to be creative - which doesn't mean you have to personally become a Banksy - but expose him to the idea that experimenting can open the door to new possibilities and skills.

Debate and encourage different opinions. The world needs inventors - people who 'think outside the box'. We need our children to think in imaginative ways to come up with different solutions. We want our children to try out new things and not be afraid. Encourage him to express his opinion and really listen to him. Often our special children have extremely valid and sensible arguments.

Following the incredible success of Team GB at the Rio Olympics in 2016, see if your child is inspired to take up a new sport or hobby.

I came across a cheeky young man named Alfie in Y5 of primary school.
He had an undiagnosed learning difficulty as he struggled with reading and writing. He had full blown angry outbursts where he threw chairs, tore up his work and ran out of class. He was hugely frustrated.

Verbally he was articulate and had fantastic general knowledge. Yet in class he was seen by his peers (and himself) as 'slow' and 'stupid'. Recognise this?
I advised his teacher to use a laptop with predictive text, specialist font and coloured paper. In addition, writing frames, word mats and topic words were readily available. His writing improved.

Yet he was still unhappy.

Then along came the Olympics in London 2012 and the amazing gymnast Louis Smith entered Alfie's world. We discovered, like Louis, Alfie had a natural skill at gymnastics. Suddenly, his peers saw him differently. His mum now puffed out with pride that he could actually achieve and he was enrolled at a local gymnastics club. And guess what? Alfie now smiles. He found his thing.

By the way, Louis Smith was diagnosed with ADHD and puts all his excess energy in training hard for Olympic glory.

66 99

The amazingly creative singer Justin Timberlake wrote "If you're a young person being called weird or different, I'm here to tell you that your critics do not count. Their words will fade. You will not."

The Rt Hon Mike Penning MP recently spoke very movingly about his battles with dyslexia at school. He said he was always in trouble and was 'written off', he was known as the 'naughty boy', and failed his 11+. He left school and joined the army where it was discovered that he had dyslexia. He'd never heard of it and thought they were telling him he had an infectious disease! Given the correct support he of course made a success of his life and is now representing the constituents of Hemel Hempstead.

The school day is jam-packed with curriculum that is required to be taught by statute. However there should be opportunities during the day for creative expression. Make sure your child is given every opportunity and then grab it with both hands!

Schools Can Damage Our Children's Emotional And Mental Health

It might be very difficult to imagine how it feels to think of yourself as useless, rubbish, no good, thick, stupid. But this is what a lot of our special children think. And whilst they're in the school system I can see why they'd think like that.

We set them up to fail. We do not provide enough opportunities for them to succeed and to feel good about themselves. Too often our special children are the ones on sanctions or punishments. They miss out the things they could achieve at or are denied opportunities to even take part.

How many times do our special children have to miss playtime because instead they're outside the Head's office because he's flicked, pinched, shouted out, thrown, got up, sat down, called out...? He is the one all staff are looking at during assembly, to glare at as soon as he mutters a word or fidgets. So the list goes on. His self-esteem is at a low ebb. Told off and missed out on the one thing he needs - freedom and space to run and move.

How do our special children feel when they see they're behind academically? They're not stupid. It's obvious to them that there is a huge chasm in ability between them and their peers.

Many of our special children are struggling not only with their own difficulties, but some are also battling with problems at home. Some children witness the most horrendous situations within their family environment. School therefore should be a safe, happy place where children can escape to and feel successful and looked after.

So it up to the schools to promote what our children can be successful at. It is vital that lessons are differentiated so that a child is given appropriate work.

That is not to say that there shouldn't be challenges - of course there should. But 'one size, fit's all' does not work for our special children.

There is far too much emphasis on the core subjects and teachers feel the pressure to raise standards. However there is space to make a child feel good about themselves. A smile, a well done, a reassurance. A gentle approach, a non-accusatory conversation. A child can instinctively feel if an adult likes them. This goes a long way to help a child feel good about themselves.

Imagine this scenario; you've gone back to school and you're required to learn to read, write and do sums in Japanese and it must be done within 6 months. However hard you try it's just not going in. You are asked to stand at the front and demonstrate what you know and answer difficult questions relating to the text. The teacher is glaring at you and all the other students can all do it easily. The teacher shakes her heads in frustration. How do you think you'd feel at this moment? Useless, stupid, incapable, a failure. Well, welcome to the world of a child with learning difficulties.

Our special children's self-worth can be at rock bottom. And school needs to take a huge amount of responsibility for this. It is completely and totally up to the institution to make all children's time at school a happy and successful one.

Ask to see the school's Behaviour Policy. What are the steps for punishment?
If your child has been sanctioned in any way find out if the correct procedures have been followed. There almost certainly should be a hierarchy of steps; starting with a simple non-verbal warning, then proceeding to missing playtime, then perhaps internal exclusion.

Make sure that a punishment is absolutely necessary for his 'crime'.

However some low level 'crimes' are completely avoidable.

See below my suggestions for teachers:

'Crime'	How to avoid it - good practice that should be happening in school
Calls out in class	Give him opportunities to share his thoughts - write his answers on a whiteboard.
Gets up out of his seat	Movement breaks, wobble cushion, latex band on his chair leg to kick.

Easily distracted	→	Sit near the front or away from others in a quiet space
Write each task in small achievable steps on a sticky note
Use a visual timetable - See the back of the book for a free offer[11]
Flicking and fiddling	→	Give him a fiddle or fidget toy such as pencil toppers or a piece of Blutak
Presentation poor	→	Let him use a laptop
Wider lines on paper
Different coloured paper
Pencil grip or triangular pencil
Left handed pen

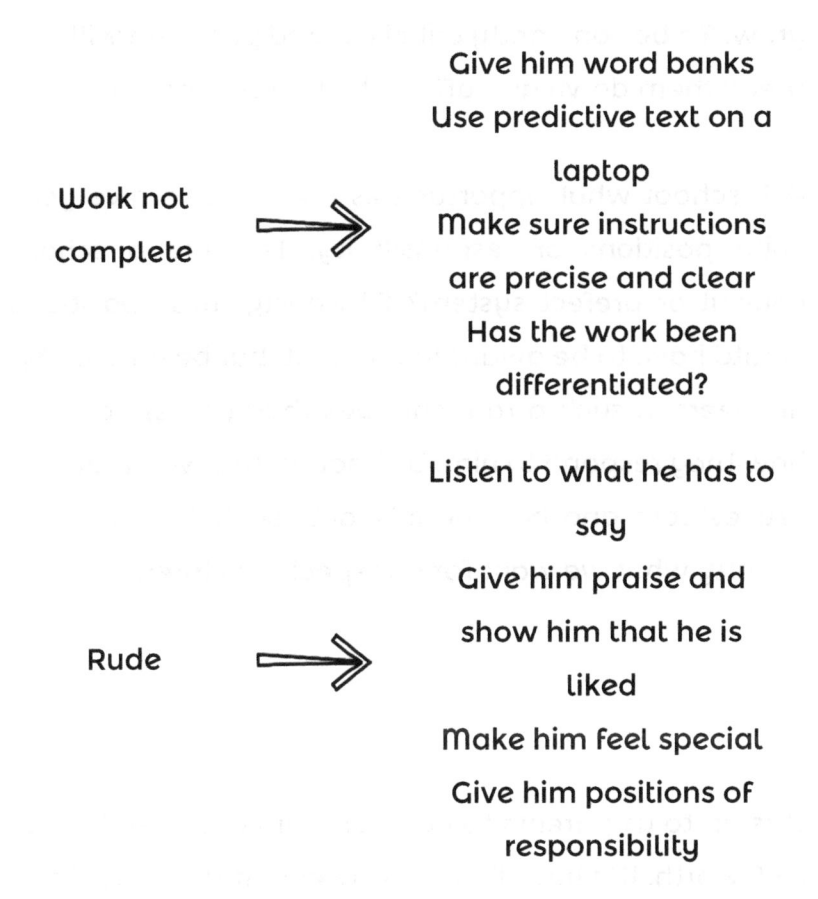

Work not complete	⟹	Give him word banks Use predictive text on a laptop Make sure instructions are precise and clear Has the work been differentiated?
Rude	⟹	Listen to what he has to say Give him praise and show him that he is liked Make him feel special Give him positions of responsibility

A child wakes up in the morning and does not say "Today I am going to be the naughtiest I can be and get shouted at so that I miss out on my playtime". On the contrary, a child is naturally curious, full of energy and hope. We must create an environment that nurtures these qualities to allow a child to flourish and grow. To be constantly criticised and punished will just break them down and affect their mental health.

Ask school what opportunities there are to give your child positions of responsibility. Is there a school council or prefect system? Obviously these positions would have to be awarded on merit, but being seen by his peers in such a role changes their perception and how they respond to him. Ultimately this will affect his self-esteem and how he interacts socially. Isn't that exactly what we want for our special children?

It is up to us parents to build up our child's feelings of self-worth. We have it in our power to make these little people feel amazing. So we need to focus on the positive and see the opportunities to make our special children feel successful.

We know our children best, so find the thing they can do without any pressure and focus on that. Heap on the praise and the smiles will follow.

That is not to say that with hard work and determination we cannot get even better. We must always aim high. Any story of a Paralympic athlete will inspire our children that despite obstacles in our way, huge success is possible.

I am a huge advocate of being outdoors. I spoke to a mum recently who hires a bouncy castle for her two children with ADHD every school holiday. She's negotiated a good deal with a local company and so she knows that her kids can bounce to their hearts' content and use up all that energy!

A note on school holidays, which can be extremely tough. I wrote on my blog 'Ten Top Tips To Survive The Summer Holiday (Without Losing Your Sanity)'[12]. The more you can plan the better. Find out from your local library what free events are on. Budget for each week and let your child work out the expenses. Give him the task of working out the cheapest options and how much left to spend (hidden maths and he wont even know). Make a project based on your child's interests, make a fact file and include photos and captions. Use everyday objects to make fun games to play together as a family. Get him to keep a journal 'My Holiday' and again include photos – or get him to make a slideshow using Powerpoint and include video.

But as much as possible, come rain or shine, go outdoors.

Find a local woods or park that they can explore, climb, get muddy, run, scream, jump, splash. Maybe organise with a group of mums who have children with similar difficulties and meet-up once a month at a park. No constraints, no judgements.

According to Mind[13] being outdoors has been proven to improve mental health, boost self-esteem, help people with mental health problems, improve physical health, and reduce social isolation. So what's not to like?

Many of you will have heard of, or been referred to, Child and Adolescent Mental Health Services (CAMHS). Depending on your postcode you may have received decent support. Unfortunately the reputation of this service is woeful and there are many parents on many forums who feel this service is pitiful. A review in

2016[14] found that 28% of children referred to CAMHS were not given access to an NHS service that could help them. Campaigns Director of Young Minds[15] has said the country is "sitting on a mental health time-bomb".

So it seems that once a child has had a diagnosis and gets into the 'system', the problems may just be exacerbated. Poor emotional and mental health is a reality. It is up to us as parents to do all we can to ensure that negative experiences at school do not compound any potential mental health issues.

A little aside, when my children were at primary school their school song was 'Everybody Can Be Somebody'. I love this sentiment. Whoever you are, wherever you've come from, whatever talent you have - you can be somebody! Beautiful.
Whilst we're on the subject of emotional and mental health, I would like to urge you to look after your own well-being.

Prince Harry in July 2016 highlighted the fact that absolutely anyone can suffer from mental health issues. So it is vital you look after yourself. Every day, and I mean every single day, you must do something for yourself.

Although our lives are hectic, frantic and can be absorbed with looking after others - we must, must, must must be kind to ourselves. Go for a walk, hum a tune, breathe deeply for 5 minutes, stare at the sky, enjoy a bar of chocolate, watch something funny on Youtube, listen to a favourite song, watch junk tv, relax in a candle-lit bath, just stop for 5 minutes.

If you can have a few hours to yourself, don't waste them on housework (the dust comes back in a week anyway). Go to the cinema, walk leisurely around the block, visit a museum or gallery, go swimming, dancing, jogging. Paint a picture, write a poem, get your nails done.

Take time for yourself. You are worth it. Do not feel guilty.

Brings to mind the analogy of an aircraft in emergency mode - you are urged to put the oxygen mask on yourself before you put it on your child. In other words, unless you're fit and healthy you are not able to support your child effectively. Look after your own emotional health and you'll have the strength to deal with the issues surrounding your child.

YOU CAN'T POUR FROM AN **EMPTY CUP** TAKE CARE OF YOURSELF FIRST.

So take this opportunity and write down 10 things you could do for yourself today.

1. _____
2. _____
3. _____
4. _____
5. _____
6. _____
7. _____
8. _____
9. _____
10. _____

Promise me you'll give yourself time today to do something just for you….

I'd like to tell you about a little boy called Jason. He has autism and finds the world confusing. When he was in Year 3 his class teacher was on probation as a newly qualified teacher. Jason would often blurt out inappropriate remarks and do the wrong thing at the wrong time. He couldn't engage with his peers and was very isolated. This inexperienced teacher would ask Jason an impossible question or get him to read aloud. I even witnessed the teacher humiliating this little lad when he couldn't give a coherent answer.

The outcome of this was that Jason became extremely anxious and tearful. He started to stutter. Maybe because the children in his class were unable to engage with him, Jason began to torment them and fight with them. All round this was an intolerable situation.

We then organised for a brilliant teaching assistant to work with Jason. She found his strengths (a love of airplanes) and he began to flourish. The class teacher was also swiftly replaced (inevitably he did not pass his training) and school life for Jason was not such a threatening place.

Consequently the stutter went away and Jason was able to achieve at his own level.

Will.i.am the incredibly talented musician and producer who has ADHD wrote "I've got all these thoughts running around in my head at the same time as I'm doing other things. I can't seem to stop or slow down. But the good news is, I know how to control it. For every obstacle there's some type of solution".

Temple Grandin author, advocate and professor with autism wrote "The thing about being autistic is that you gradually get less and less autistic, because you keep learning, you keep learning how to behave. It's like being in a play; I'm always in a play."

Emotional and mental health is fragile. Too many adults are affected by feelings of low self-esteem, poor self-worth. And this can begin in childhood. So it is up to us as a society to help all our children, but particularly our vulnerable special children, to feel good about themselves. This means enveloping them with praise, kindness and a sense of 'everybody can be somebody'.

#4

Targets Matter Too Much

And so we come to the dreaded targets. Oh where to start...?

When I was at primary school in the 1960s and 1970s it was quite fun. From memory, we did a lot of fun stuff like making a 3D model of the school building, music, sewing a bookmark, playing the recorder, trip to Verulamium, netball club, choir, 5 day visit to Holland and Belgium, country dancing, maypole dancing, sports day where I ran relay, house teams (I was in Churchill), playing 'kiss chase' on the field! I also remember a bit of the work side of things, Alpha and Beta maths where we just worked on our own trying to figure out how to do the pesky sums. New Worlds to Conquer, a comprehension text book which we plodded through unaided and learning joined-up handwriting. The teachers sat at their desk and didn't move except to the blackboard to scrape with chalk something for us to copy. This certainly is not the education utopia, but my own school days, as I remember them, filled me with joy and taught me the basics.

But roll forward 30 years from today. What will our children remember about school? Perhaps Year 6 will remember spending practically the whole year to May practicing Standard Assessment Tests (SATs) to the detriment of any other fun stuff. The 6 year olds in Year 2 may remember that they had to learn adverbials, prepositional phrases and phonemes.

Now I'm not suggesting fun things don't happen nowadays, because they do. But the major emphasis is on the SATs and the targets that have been set. There is so much pressure on everyone for these targets to be reached that the important peripheral stuff has almost become superfluous. Every hour of the school day pre-SATs is set aside to practice, practice, practice. Children have huge expectations on them to reach the expected level. The irony is that at the time of writing, we are not quite sure what the 'expected' level actually is. Nicky Morgan the Secretary of State for Education devised a new system for measuring, scrapped the previous levels of 1 to 6 and set a new benchmark of 100. Unfortunately for her (she's since be reshuffled) only 53%[16] of children reached this level. Woops. Need a new system!

Michael Rosen[17], the fabulous former Children's Poet Laureate and novelist, is a long-time critic of the current system. He wrote in August 2016 that the SATs were a "disgrace" and that *"...it was nonsense used as a means of measuring teachers' ability to teach nonsense."*

Will our children remember the fun things? I really hope so. Time will tell.

SATs are here to stay. The Government loves to measure, compare and contrast. But as a parent, you are entitled to ask if the fun stuff is happening too. As I have already expressed, our special children flourish in an environment where they are successful. So if learning times tables is their thing then great but there must also be plenty of other opportunities for them to learn and grow.

If you are dissatisfied contact Chair of Governors for the school. Their number will be available through the school website or local council. Or consider becoming a Governor yourself, that way you will really see the inner workings of the institution and have the opportunity to express your opinions.

I know you feel the pressure too but please do not take SATs home. Please try to avoid getting a tutor or buying the papers to practice. He gets enough practice at school.

Instead use your time at home to do the fun stuff. You know. Playing, reading, laughing, make a den, make a play, and make a mess. Visit the local library and borrow ten books on a range of interests. Have a water fight.

Introduce maths concepts in things you do together, cooking, going to the shops, measuring boxes to make a model. Include rich language, ask for opinions, debate and encourage discussion.
Honestly, your time at home will be so full there will be not a second to think about SATs.

A gorgeous little girl called Chloe struggles hugely in class. She has ADHD and fidgets, calls out, is easily distracted, has messy writing and rarely finishes her work. She is not motivated and has poor self-image. She is always in trouble for one thing or another. Yet she is an amazing horse rider and her family have given her responsibility to look after her own horse. We used this as a springboard and encouraged her to write about her horse, instructions, lists, invitations. She had a budget that she could use to buy supplies and maths sort of now makes sense. She is yet to take her SATs but I can guarantee that she won't reach the desired standard (whatever that may be). But take a look at her personalised project and you'll see what standard she really is. Gold standard all the way.

Daniel Radcliffe, best known for his lead role as Harry Potter, was having a "hard time in school" due to his dyspraxia so his mum introduced him to acting. Look at him now…..he hasn't done too badly!

Steven Spielberg, the dyslexic director of incredible films such as Schindler's List and Saving Private Ryan advised students with dyslexia that "sometimes you must dart between the raindrops to get where you want to go."

We will not be able to erase SATs from the curriculum. Whatever Government is in place they are well and truly embedded. On a positive note, the National Curriculum has streamlined education across the country and targets have ensured that we teach to high standards. This should be praised as we want to aim high and produce well educated young people.

We must however be mindful that there is more to an education than a solid understanding of core subjects. There are the elements of fun, personal growth, sense of self-worth, belonging, and preparedness for society, achievement and social awareness.

Can you imagine living in a society where all are valued for their skills and character; rather than a sense of failure which our current system foists upon us?

#5

There's A Real World Out There

The world has changed. Jobs that our children will be working in don't even exist yet. Who could have possibly imagined that there would be a job entitled 'Android UX Engineer'? Sounds like it's from fictional story from Star Trek but it's a real job working for YouTube.

So are we preparing our children for this new world life? Actually, no.

Primary schools are far behind in technology and modern thinking. We strangely still worry about handwriting. Loops, tails and joins. Why? We all use laptops to write letters. Scrap that. We don't even write letters. We email. Yes it is lovely to receive a handwritten note - that should be encouraged. But do we really need to dedicate precious time at school to teach handwriting. And it gets better. Children are tested in their SATs for the quality of their handwriting. Bonkers!

The world needs thinkers, innovators, entrepreneurs. But are we preparing our children for these roles? No, no, no! And guess who the ones who are able to 'think outside the box?' Our beautiful, special children who have had to side step and deal with failure, dodge difficult questions, find innovative ways to cope. It is well know that dyslexic adults are able to problem-solve creatively[18]. They become architects and engineers, actors and inventors.

So what are we doing to encourage this behaviour in school? Not a lot.

Again the curriculum is so tightly woven around the academic skills surrounding SATs that there is little room for free thinking, creativity and expression. Poetry is prescriptive and creative writing is stifled. There is no opportunity for our older children to make models - unless it is raining and the Lego box is pounced on. Our future builders and designers have absolutely no chance in primary school of developing their skills. Our special children again who have the opportunities to shine are denied their moment in the spotlight.

And what about real-life skills such as money management. Our special children will go out into the real world with the temptation of huge loans, hire purchase agreements and the desire for shiny new things now. We need to educate our children from an early age that if you want something special you must earn it and save for it. Parents are already great at this. We give our children chores and get them to save for a treat.

But what are our primary schools doing to encourage financial prudence? We teach in the classrooms how to recognise coins, how to use times tables to problem-solve shopping scenarios. But nothing surrounding the morality of spending or the benefits of saving. Unfortunately it is our vulnerable special children who will be caught out in the credit card, debt-ridden traps.

Where else in life are we constrained so much by time? Write this amazing poem in 10 minutes as it's time for play /assembly / lunch. Come on. Be creative. Too much pressure in an unnatural situation.

As adults in the real world, we give ourselves time to complete a task. We allow creativity to flow naturally. We have the option of walking away or stopping if we are unable to focus or the idea just isn't coming or we just can't fathom out how to put the IKEA drawers together. But no such luxury within the confines of a school day. Too little time with too much curriculum to cover. There is certainly no time to reflect. Quick off to maths.

Ask school to promote schemes such as Young Enterprise[19] - teaching children about money, business and competition.

Ask at school what opportunities your child has for exploring and building. Are there after-school or lunchtime clubs? Could you get a group of parents to organise one?

Lego[20] are exploring ways to enhance the teaching of Maths and English in schools. Bring this to the attention of the class teacher.

Encourage local businesses to visit the school. Many successful entrepreneurs will tell you that they didn't do well at school as had an undiagnosed special need. They commonly have spirit and determination to succeed and have had to use problem-solving skills to survive. The reality of failure and trying again in a different way are all attributes they've needed in business. For our special children to hear their story and know that it is possible to succeed can be motivational and life-changing.

And how do you think our special children would respond to a Paralympic athlete visiting the school? One of the legacies[21] of London 2012 Olympics was for these amazing men and women to share the dream and to inspire the next generation. To see someone with a physical difficulty overcome huge obstacles to achieve at the highest level cannot fail to motivate. Ian Rose came to visit my school and what an impact he made on the 700 strong audience. After being born with childhood eye cancer, Ian lost his left eye and most of the sight in his right. But with the support of his family he went onto become Judo champion of GB. If his story just touched one of our special children to feel that there are no limits, then job well done.

Give your child as many all-round experiences as possible. Don't rely on school to prepare your child for the outside, real world. Obviously we don't want to scare our children and burden them with adult problems, but we need them to learn to take choices and be responsible.

So give him many opportunities to take responsibilities at home - don't do everything for him. Let him do for jobs around the house, putting his things away, choosing activities, places to go. Use a visual timetable so that he can do this independently. I'm offering you a free DVD (plus P+P) to download original graphics and grids to make your own resource. See back of the book for details.

During holidays give him a budget. He can work out daily expenditure and how to earn any extra money. Encourage him to save up for a desired item but when the money's gone, it's gone.

Give your child a clear message. There will be many opportunities where he will be successful. With hard work, motivation and a great attitude, as well as support and encouragement, there are huge possibilities for success. The world needs free thinkers, inventors, entrepreneurs, engineers, sales, trades, drivers, dancers, artists, educators, hairstylists, designers, computer analysts and entertainers. There is a place for everyone. We just need to help our special children find their place.

A young lad called Jake had been diagnosed as severely dyslexic. He found work extremely challenging. His self-esteem was low yet he's very bright, articulate and had a great general knowledge and clear ideas and opinions. But he compared himself to his peers who were all able to read and write with ease. He hated the fact that he relied on a support assistant and that he was lumped together with the other specials in the class. The school had been great, providing him with specialist teacher input, coloured overlays, specialist reading books, coloured paying, speech software. He was still stuck. So we kept trying. There always is the one thing that makes a difference. For Jake this was the quite expensive purchase of an amazing gadget that scans the text and reads it back via headphones. Jake found his independence and was less reliant on an assistant which boosted his confidence. Jake will need to find a job eventually and support himself. He is bright and capable. But school doesn't suit him. The constraints of the classroom, coupled with his severe learning difficulty, means he will always be struggling. I know that once he leaves school, he will immerse himself in a trade and be highly successful. We just need to make sure his time within the institution is managed carefully, to allow him to feel valued and included.

❝ ❞

Louise Mensch, author and former MP "With ADHD your whole focus is on what you are good at, which is why I loved politics but couldn't keep my bedroom tidy.
You are great at what you are good at, but incredibly scatterbrained when it comes to anything else".

Jamie Oliver, chef and renowned advocate of healthy eating in children, was diagnosed with dyslexia as an

adult. *"It was with great regret that I didn't do better at school.*
People just thought I was thick, it was a struggle, I never really had anyone to help and who could bring out my strengths."

The school system does not prepare our special children for the realities of the real world. We can put pressure on the school to provide opportunities but unfortunately I think this area is down to us parents. Until the Government changes the National Curriculum model and releases time back to teachers to teach real stuff, this will not change.

Conclusion – Together We Can Bring About Change

Teachers today are doing a brilliant job. When I started teaching in 1986 pre-National Curriculum, SATs and Ofsted, I more or less was left to my own devices and could decide for myself what I wanted to teach. There was little scrutiny. This was not a great system and it needed streamlining.

Fast forward to today. Our teachers are amazing, incredible and dedicated. But frazzled. The demands are over-whelming - testing, targets, reports, marking, planning, teaching. They are multi-tasking all day long with a class of 30 individuals. They are social workers, peacemakers, carers and educators specialising in sports, arts and history. Quite a task! Most are doing a great job.

But put into the mix our special children and the huge extra demands this places on a teacher and it is little wonder why some of our special children's needs are just not being met.

Parents need to be more involved. In fact Brian Lamb, heading the Lamb Inquiry[22] stated *"I have seen for myself the difference that schools can make with good information, and particularly with good communication: the engagement of parents for the benefit of their child's progress; trust in place of conflict."*

Evidence (as well as common sense) suggests that the more involved you are with the school, the more your children will be successful. I hope this book has given you plenty of ammunition to discuss with the school what needs to be done, so our special children succeed.

But please do not create an atmosphere of 'them and us'. If our children pick up on any animosity towards school or they hear you being negative towards their class teacher, it may impact on their behaviour at school. Of course you may feel like screaming and shouting from the roof tops – but please try to keep this away from your child as much as possible.

So what is the way forward?

To me, the answer is clear:

- ✓ Better training for teachers how to successfully include and differentiate for all of our special children
- ✓ Better training for teachers in learning about dyslexia, autism, ADHD, Asperger's and behaviour management
- ✓ Parents and school to work as a partnership
- ✓ More funding to allow additional staff in schools to support in class, as well as specialists who are able to plan for great inclusion
- ✓ Creative curriculum which allows teachers to combine all areas of interest into a school day to allow all children to shine

It is time to contact your MP. We must make a fuss about this broken system and how our special children are being failed time and time again. Our Governments must see from first-hand experiences that there needs to be change and more funding. Find your MP on Twitter and tweet them daily until they respond. Again keep it polite and full of facts. Write to them at their surgery address - you can Google their contact details. Talking of Twitter. Send your messages with the hashtag #warriormums. Let's get this trending and make a noise.

I have set up a petition[23] for the attention of Justine Greening, Secretary of State for Education. The petition '*Teachers to be trained in ADHD and how to effectively support children in the classroom*' can be found at change.org. The direct link is at the back of the book.

Training is woefully inadequate with 'Special Needs' taught as a whole unit, for as little as half a day, with ADHD given lip service. A child with ADHD can cause huge disruption in the classroom if their behaviour is not managed correctly. You would have thought adequate training would be given priority.

If there was a better understanding of specific special needs and what to do about it, perhaps there wouldn't be so many of our wonderful, talented special children feeling like they've failed and that society has given up on them. If a teacher has the skills to include and differentiate, then we are actively helping our special children to feel confident and succeed. I urge you to sign my petition and share, share, share.

Or start your own petition[24] and promote it on social media - send your MP the link too. If you get 100,000 signatures it must be considered for debate in Parliament by law. If we all put on the pressure, then who knows...

We are on our way.

I have presented five reasons why school fails your child with special needs - but I am hopeful.

I see that teachers are waking up to the notion that if there is change within a classroom, then there will be change within a child. I have personally witnessed time and time again, that with small, simple modifications, techniques and strategies we can make a massive difference to the emotional well-being of a child. How great is that?

If our special children are unable to access our world - then we need to reach into theirs.

If a child cannot learn in the way we teach, we must teach in a way that the child can learn.

About The Author

Soli Lazarus B.Educ (Hons) Psychology

Soli's son has ADHD so knows what it's like as a parent to struggle on a daily basis and feel isolated.

Soli was an Assistant SENCO, an Inclusion Specialist and a fully qualified teacher with some 30 years experience; specialising in ADHD, Autism, Developmental Delay, Communication and Learning Difficulties, Down Syndrome and Dyslexia. She had a senior role in a London mainstream primary school and attended numerous SEN courses and exhibitions. Soli ran workshops, training and planning for inclusion sessions.

Soli set up Yellow Sun, a consultancy to support parents who are struggling with the behaviour of their special needs children. She offers practical advice support and one-to-one coaching. She also delivers training online where parents can learn techniques and strategies in the comfort of their own home and in their own time. She has produced a resource 'The Secret To Behaviour Success'.

Soli runs a monthly support group called Warrior Mums Club where mums come together to swap stories, get support and feel like they are not battling alone. There is no criticism, blame or judgement.

Soli has also written an online course to help families live a happy life with a child with ADHD and has launched a membership club. All details on the website www.soli-lazarus.com

Soli is involved in an All Party Parliamentary Group of MPs looking at what better provision can be put in place for children and adults with ADHD. She has been interviewed on TV, for numerous podcasts and writes for SEN publications.

About The Author

She is very happily married to Steven and has two lovely grown up children David and Rosie. Soli lives in London.

Resources Available From Yellow Sun

- ✓ 1:1 Tailored support to help manage your child's challenging behaviour. For more details www.isupportyou.me.uk
- ✓ Monthly informal meetings where mums come together to offer support, guidance and friendship. Membership to Warrior Mums' Club can be booked at www.meetandsupport.uk
- ✓ Visual timetables can be used to help your child manage his day and avoid tantrums and meltdowns. www.visual-timetable.com
- ✓ Free training videos 'Live a Happy Life With ADHD' www.liveahappylifewithadhd.com/freetraining
- ✓ Read Soli's blog www.soli-lazarus.com/blog

Connect With Yellow Sun

Facebook www.facebook.com/yellowsunsoli

Twitter www.twitter.com/soli_yellowsun

Contact soli@yellow-sun.com

References

[1] Department of Education Ref SFR 26/2014 http://bit.ly/1EDLJ1X

[2] June 2016 The Key, which provides leadership and management support to schools.
Findings:
- 82% of mainstream schools in England do not have sufficient funding and budget to adequately provide for pupils with SEND
- Three-quarters of schools have pupils who have been waiting longer than expected for assessment of special educational needs or an education, health and care plan
- 88% of school leaders think initial teacher training does not adequately prepare teachers to support pupils with SEND http://bit.ly/2aNuAYO

[3] Standards and Testing Agency Guidance for SATs and recommended levels of assessment http://bit.ly/1jk6zvA

[4] Clicker – a great tool for reading and writing http://bit.ly/2agaKVt

References

[5] Numicon – colourful visual pieces to help with maths. See this YouTube clip which explains all http://bit.ly/2ai26Va

[6] Free games to download. These are totally free and my gift to you. Go to website https://isupportyou.me.uk/free-games

[7] Amazon audio books https://www.amazon.co.uk

[8] Chickenshed Inclusive Theatre Company https://www.chickenshed.org.uk/

[9] Penniwells Horse Riding For The Disabled http://www.penniwellsrda.com/

[10] The Programme for International Student Assessment (PISA) is an international survey that occurs every three years which aims to evaluate education systems worldwide by testing the skills and knowledge of 15-year-old students. Results published by OECD

[11] Visual timetables can be used to help your child manage his day. For your free copy (plus P+P) visit www.visual-timetable.com

[12] 'Ten Top Tips To Survive The Summer Holiday (Without Losing Your Sanity)' www.warrior-mums.com

[13] Mind October 2013 'Feel Better Outside, Feel Better Inside' a report including new findings from the University of Essex showing the many benefits of ecotherapy for mental wellbeing http://bit.ly/2alscdE

[14] Anne Longfield, Government's children's commissioner for England found that 28% of children referred to CAMHS services from all sources – including parents, schools, social workers and hospitals – were not given access to an NHS service that could help them http://bit.ly/2avsuhc

[15] Lucie Russell, Campaigns Director of Young Minds http://bit.ly/2alscdE

[16] Key stage 2 results for 2016 http://bit.ly/29eCCY8

[17] Michael Rosen poet and author http://bit.ly/2awIRZm

[18] Education Influences Creativity in Dyslexic and Non-Dyslexic Children and Teenagers http://bit.ly/2aCTScK

[19] Young Enterprise is the UK's leading charity that empowers young people to harness their personal and business skills https://www.young-enterprise.org.uk/

[20] Lego Education for primary schools http://lego.build/2aiX8e2

[21] **Paralympic Education Programme** http://bit.ly/2agTGys

[22] **Lamb Inquiry 2009** http://bit.ly/2cid6Hv

[23] **Sign and share my petition 'Teachers to be trained in ADHD and how to effectively support pupils in the classroom'** http://chn.ge/2bAlYHE

[24] **Start your own petition** https://www.change.org/en-GB